Is it a bat?

Written by Karra McFarlane

Collins

It is red and fat.

Is it a hen?

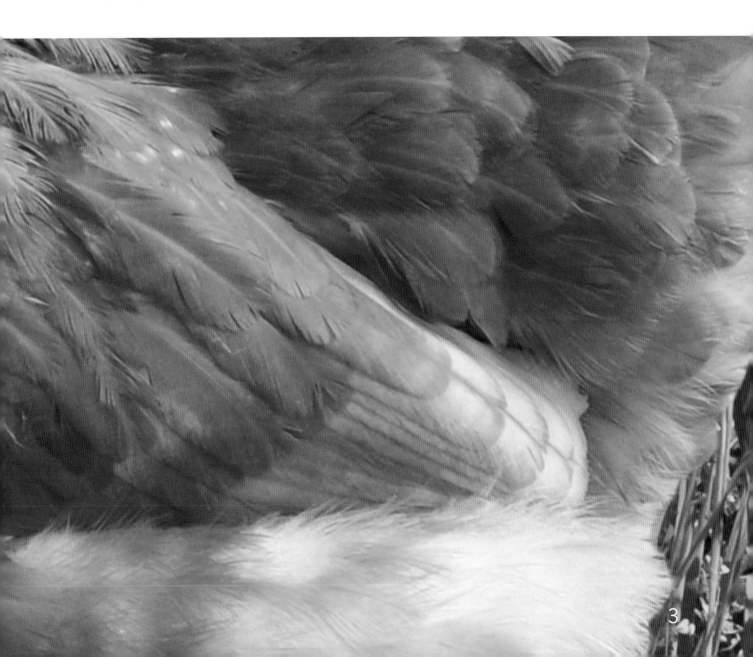

It is a hen.

A big fat red hen.

It runs in the mud!

Is it a dog?

It is a dog.

The fit dog runs off.

It is big and red.

Is it a big bat?

It is a big bat.

It naps in the sun.

/o/

14

/g/

15

 After reading

Letters and Sounds: Phase 2

Word count: 56

Focus phonemes: /f/ /h/ /b/ /g/ /o/ /e/ /u/ /r/ ff

Common exception words: is, the

Curriculum links: Understanding the World

Early learning goals: Reading: use phonic knowledge to decode regular words and read them aloud accurately, read some common irregular words

Developing fluency

- Your child may enjoy hearing you read the book.
- Model reading one of the questions with the appropriate intonation. Now ask your child to read the pages with questions on, while you read the other pages.

Phonic practice

- Support your child in reading CVC words. Look at the word **dog**. Ask your child to sound talk and blend the word d/o/g.
- Now ask them to do the same with the following words:

    red   hen   bat   sun   fit   big

- Look at the "I spy sounds" pages (14–15). Say the sounds together. How many items can your child spot that contain the /o/ sound in them (e.g. *dog, jog, oranges, pond*), or the /g/ sound in them? (e.g. *goat, dogs, jug, jog, geese, grapes*)

Extending vocabulary

- Look at pages 4 to 5 together. Point out that the hen is described as **big**, **fat** and **red**. Ask your child if they can think of any other words to describe the hen. (e.g. *brown, fluffy*)
- Look at pages 8 to 9 together. Point out that the dog is described as **fit**. Ask your child if they can think of any other words to describe the dog. (e.g. *fast, wet, white*)